1-10-06

Landmark
Events in
American
History

The Settling of
St. Augustine

Janet Riehecky

WORLD ALMANAC® LIBRARY

Please visit our web site at: www.worldalmanaclibrary.com
For a free color catalog describing World Almanac® Library's list of high-quality
books and multimedia programs, call 1-800-848-2928 (USA) or 1-800-387-3178
(Canada). World Almanac® Library's fax: (414) 332-3567.

Library of Congress Cataloging-in-Publication Data

Riehecky, Janet, 1953-
    The settling of St. Augustine / by Janet Riehecky.
        p. cm. — (Landmark events in American history)
    Includes bibliographical references and index.
    Summary: Traces the history of St. Augustine, Florida, from its founding and development
as a Spanish colony and military outpost in 1565 through the early eighteenth century, and
discusses the impact of European colonialization on the native Timucuan Indians.
    ISBN 0-8368-5376-8 (lib. bdg.)
    ISBN 0-8368-5404-7 (softcover)
    1. Saint Augustine (Fla.)—History—Juvenile literature. 2. Spaniards—Florida—Saint
Augustine—History—Juvenile literature. 3. Timucua Indians—Florida—Saint Augustine—
History—Juvenile literature. 4. Florida—History—To 1821—Juvenile literature. [1. Saint
Augustine (Fla.)—History. 2. Spaniards—Florida—Saint Augustine—History. 3. Timucua
Indians. 4. Indians of North America—Florida. 5. Florida—History—To 1821.] I. Title.
II. Series.
F319.S2R54   2003
975.9'18—dc21   2002033158

First published in 2003 by
World Almanac® Library
330 West Olive Street, Suite 100
Milwaukee, WI 53212 USA

Copyright © 2003 by World Almanac® Library.

Produced by Discovery Books
Editor: Sabrina Crewe
Designer and page production: Sabine Beaupré
Photo researcher: Sabrina Crewe
Maps and diagrams: Stefan Chabluk
World Almanac® Library editorial direction: Mark J. Sachner
World Almanac® Library art direction: Tammy Gruenewald
World Almanac® Library production: Jessica Yanke

Photo credits: Corbis: cover, pp. 4, 7, 14, 15, 16, 18, 20, 22, 23, 24, 25, 26, 28, 29, 30,
35, 37 (top), 38, 39, 40, 41; The Granger Collection: pp. 13, 31, 34; North Wind Picture
Archives: pp. 5, 6, 8, 9, 10, 11, 12, 17, 19, 27, 32, 33, 37 (bottom), 42, 43.

Printed in the United States of America

1 2 3 4 5 6 7 8 9 07 06 05 04 03

Contents

Introduction

A view of St. Augustine today from just off the Florida coast. St. Augustine has grown from a tiny settlement that struggled for survival into a prosperous city.

A Spanish Settlement

In March 1565, King Philip II of Spain signed a contract with sailor and explorer Pedro Menéndez de Avilés. The contract authorized Menéndez to found a settlement in the land of Florida in North America.

Spain already had large, flourishing **colonies** in Central and South America and on islands in the Caribbean Sea, but it had yet to establish any north of Mexico. King Philip was hopeful that the Florida region would produce valuable **natural resources**, as South America had done.

On September 8, 1565, Menéndez landed in Florida at the site of the Native village of Seloy. There, his men built a settlement that Menéndez named St. Augustine. Today, St. Augustine is the oldest existing European settlement in the United States of America.

The European Impact

The establishment of the city of St. Augustine marked the beginning of the Spanish conquest of the part of America that would later become the United States. As a result of that conquest, no aspect of life in the region remained unchanged. The culture, social and political structure, **economy**, and lifestyle of the original Native people were destroyed. Even the environment changed as a result of the introduction of new species of plants and animals.

Struggles in the Colony

The Spanish colonists in St. Augustine faced incredible hardships, but they survived. St. Augustine became an important port for Spanish ships carrying goods from other colonies. The city established courts of law, businesses, and an education system many years before there were any British colonies in North America.

St. Augustine became the first truly international North American city. The flags of four nations flew over it at one time or another in its long history. Spanish, French, British, Africans, and Latin Americans all lived there in addition to the Native population. Each culture left its mark on St. Augustine and what is now the state of Florida. St. Augustine also played a part in many wars: These include the French and Indian War, the American Revolution, the Seminole Wars, and the American Civil War.

Before the Spanish arrived, Florida was a heavily forested region with a traditional society that had existed for thousands of years. This is a reconstruction of a shelter built by the Timucuan people who inhabited the St. Augustine area long before European settlement.

Before the Europeans

The People of Florida

Native Americans lived in Florida for thousands of years before Europeans came to North America. In the early 1500s, about twelve different Indian groups lived in what are now northern Florida and southern Georgia. These peoples had their own governments and differing customs and languages.

The people who lived near present-day St. Augustine called themselves the Saturiba. Europeans, however, used the name Timucuan Indians—a name given by the French in 1564—for all Native groups in northern Florida. Southern Florida held a number of other peoples, including the Ais, Tequesta, and Calusa. In the present-day **panhandle** of Florida were the Apalache. To the north, in what is now southern Georgia, were the Guale people.

These Florida men are training for various sports, including running races and competing with bow and arrow. In the foreground, a group plays a game in which a ball is thrown up to hit a square on a post, like basketball without the basket.

Chiefs and Councils

The Timucuan Indians in the St. Augustine area were organized into chiefdoms consisting of a group of villages ruled by a great chief.

In addition to the great chief, each Timucuan village had its own chief and council. The office of chief would pass from the current chief to his nephew, the oldest son of his oldest sister. If his sister didn't have a son, her oldest daughter would become chief.

The Village

The number of villages in a chiefdom could range from two to forty or more. Each village might contain as many as two hundred houses. Timucuan villages were sometimes protected by a surrounding fence made of long poles.

In the center of each village stood a large structure called the council house. The chief lived there, and it was also used for council and other meetings.

Ordinary houses in Timucuan villages were round or oval, about 20 or 25 feet (6 to 7.6 meters) across, and made of **saplings** stuck into the ground and bent inward to form a domed roof. People wove plants around the saplings to make walls, and the walls and roof were then covered with **thatch** made from palm leaves.

There were two holes, one for a door and the other designed to let out smoke through the roof.

Some historians think the Timucuans lived in their villages only eight or nine months a year, while their crops were growing. During the winter, they might have moved to temporary hunting camps.

In this picture of agricultural workers in Florida, men are preparing the ground while a woman drills holes for corn seed. Another woman sows the seed.

Timucuan society had a strict class system. People belonged to a clan that was classed as royalty, nobility, or common. Chiefs always came from the royal class. Council members were from the nobility, and the lowest class comprised ordinary workers.

What They Wore

Because of the warm climate in Florida, Timucuans wore little clothing, usually just a loincloth or skirt made of deerskin. Both men and women wore their hair long, but men tied theirs up on top of their heads. If a warrior died, his widow cut off her hair and left it on his grave. She could not remarry until her short hair grew back to shoulder length.

Florida people wore bird feathers and necklaces of shells, pearls, or fish teeth. Men also wore earrings and plates of gold, silver, or brass on their legs. Both men and women decorated their bodies with paint for ceremonies.

Farmers and Hunters

Timucuan people spent much of their time getting food. The men hunted for deer, rabbits, and alligators and caught a wide variety of fish from oceans and rivers. Both men and women farmed. Men prepared the ground and women did the planting. Corn was their most important crop, but beans, squash, and pumpkins were also planted in the same fields. In addition, women and children gathered wild berries, nuts, oysters, clams, and birds' eggs.

Spiritual Ceremonies

Timucuans gave honor to the Sun as the source of life. Their priests led ceremonies of worship before hunting trips or on other significant occasions. In a ceremony to welcome spring, the body of a stag, with the horns still on, was stuffed with herbs. It was then hung on a high tree, facing east, as an offering to the Sun.

Hunting Deer

"The Indians, when hunting deer, . . . fitted the skins of the largest deer that they have been able to catch over their bodies so that the deer's head covered their own and they were able to look through the eye holes as if it were a mask. . . . There were a lot of deer in that region so they were easily able to shoot them with their bows and arrows. . . . They were able to remove the deer skin and prepare it without any metal knife, just shells, with such skill that I doubt there was anyone in the whole of Europe who could do it better."

From the journal of French artist Jacques Le Moyne, 1564

Chapter 2

Arrival of the Spanish

Bimini

In the years following Christopher Columbus's journey to the Americas in 1492, Spanish colonies had been established in the Caribbean. One explorer, Juan Ponce de León, had settled and become governor of the island of Puerto Rico in 1509.

From the people of Puerto Rico, Ponce de León heard stories of an island of great wealth called Bimini, north of Cuba. Bimini, they claimed, had a spring whose waters restored youth to the drinker. Ponce de León reported this to Spain, suggesting he lead an expedition to find it. In 1512, Spain granted Ponce de León permission to locate, conquer, and colonize Bimini.

The Naming of Florida

On March 3, 1513, Ponce de León set sail with three ships, heading

This picture shows the men of Ponce de León's 1513 expedition drinking the water of a Florida spring. It is more probable, however, that they were looking for gold than for the fountain of youth.

Landing in Florida

". . . the second of April, sailing West-northwest, the water went diminishing to nine fathoms, at one league from land, . . . they ran along the coast seeking harbor, and that night they anchored close to land, in eight fathoms of water. And thinking this land was an island, they called it Florida."

Antonio de Herrera y Tordesillas, writing about Ponce de León's landing, General History of the Acts of the Castilians in the Islands and Mainland of the Ocean Sea, *1601*

Where Did Ponce de León Land?

Historians argue over the exact spot of Juan Ponce de León's landing, but a good argument can be made that it was at the site of St. Augustine. In 1868, some large stones were uncovered there, arranged in the shape of a cross and buried next to a spring. The cross contains fifteen stones lying east to west and thirteen lying north to south. In Spanish tradition, this would mean 1513, the year of Ponce de León's landing.

northwest from Puerto Rico. On Easter Sunday, March 27, lookouts on board the ships sighted land along the eastern coast of Florida. Ponce de León named the land *Pascua Florida*, Spanish for "flowery Easter." On April 2, the expedition went ashore.

It is likely that other European explorers and slave ships landed in Florida before this, but Ponce de León is credited with Florida's "discovery." Although he didn't locate the riches of Bimini or a fountain of youth, Ponce de León did make a valuable find: the Gulf Stream. This swiftly running current within the waters of the Atlantic Ocean provided a speedy path for ships traveling to Spain with gold and silver from Central and South America.

The Spanish **Empire** included places much more profitable than Florida. In the Caribbean, the city of Havana on the island of Cuba was a busy port and center for Spanish trade from the early 1500s.

A Spanish ship anchors on the Florida coast during the early 1500s. The first explorers and colonists did not make much headway against Florida's environment nor with its Native people.

Attempts at Colonization

Florida became the northernmost piece of land claimed by the Spanish Empire in the Americas. It was never considered an important part of the empire, but Spain did make several attempts to explore and colonize it.

In 1521, Ponce de León led an expedition to explore and settle on the west coast of Florida. He died of an arrow wound, and his colony failed. In 1528, Pánfilo de Narváez led four hundred men into the interior, searching for gold. Only four men survived that expedition. More expeditions followed, all ending in disaster.

Most often it was the Spaniards' own attitudes that defeated them. The Spanish regarded all Indians as savages and assumed their own way of doing things was superior. Instead of learning from local people how best to live in a new environment, Spaniards attempted to recreate Spanish villages. They made inadequate preparations for feeding their people, expecting locals to provide them with food. They refused to adapt their heavy clothing to the humid climate.

Taking Slaves

During the first half of the sixteenth century, Spanish ships landed frequently on the coast of Florida so that soldiers could capture Indians and sell them into slavery in Spanish colonies. They sometimes engaged in trade with Native people, but they also took by force anything they wanted. Not surprisingly, the people of Florida fought back, attacking Spanish soldiers and explorers. Sometimes they misdirected the Spaniards, telling them there was gold to the north or west just to get rid of them. In the years prior to the 1560s, the people of Florida succeeded in forcing invaders to leave.

European Contact

In the long run, however, it was the Native people who lost out in the conflict with Europeans. Historians are not sure how many Timucuans there were before Europeans came to North America. Estimates range as high as 200,000. Whatever the number, contact with Europeans resulted in the population being wiped out.

The Spanish and other settlers from Europe brought diseases to which Native people had never been exposed. Epidemics raged through Florida, killing whole villages. Violent Spaniards killed many other people. Those who resisted Spanish rule were often sold as slaves or killed. Some estimates say that as many as 90 percent of the Timucuan people died within decades of the first European contact. In 1717, a **census** listed only about 250 Timucuans. By the end of the 1700s, there were none at all.

Hernando de Soto, shown here on horseback, came to Florida to find gold after gaining great wealth in Peru. On an expedition that began in 1639, de Soto and his soldiers captured and killed Native people and spread disease among Florida villages.

Founding the Settlement

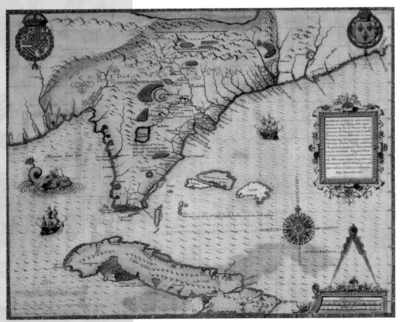

The Florida region in the 1500s and 1600s was much bigger than the state of Florida today. This early map showing Florida (yellow) and Cuba (green) was taken from the drawings of Jacques Le Moyne, an artist and mapmaker who was part of an unsuccessful French colony in the 1500s.

In 1561, the latest failure of a colony in Florida led King Philip II of Spain to declare that there would be no more expeditions there. For some years, that ban held. In early 1565, however, the king began negotiating with Pedro Menéndez de Avilés to found a Spanish colony in Florida. A contract was signed on March 20.

The French Arrive First

Ten days later, King Philip learned that France had sent an expedition to Florida to build a fort and start a colony. When he heard this, King Philip told Menéndez to destroy the settlement on arrival. Spain did not want the French colonizing Florida or establishing a base from which to attack Spanish ships.

Catholics and Protestants

Before 1517, there were many Catholics who were unhappy with the corruption in the Catholic Church. After a protest in 1517 led by German priest Martin Luther, churches were founded separately from the Catholic establishment. The protesting Christians became known as Protestants.

The conflict between Catholics and Protestants was intense. In many cases their hostility led to civil wars. In Spain, people suspected of being Protestants were often tortured and killed.

The Huguenots at Fort Caroline protected themselves with a triangular wooden wall surrounded by a moat. Even so, they were attacked by local Native people who resented the French presence on their land.

There were also religious reasons for King Philip's order. The Spanish were determined to stop the spread of Protestantism both in Spain and elsewhere. And the French settlers were Lutheran Protestants, known as Huguenots in France.

Fort Caroline

The Huguenots landed in Florida early in 1564 at the mouth of the St. Johns River, near the present-day city of Jacksonville. They built Fort Caroline, home to about three hundred soldiers, sailors, and craftsmen. The settlers soon faced the problems of most North American colonists: starvation, disease, and conflict with local people. In the summer of 1565, the Huguenots were considering abandoning the colony.

Extreme Famine

"We were constrained to endure extreme famine, which continued among us all the month of May . . . we were constrained to eat roots. . . . Yea, this misery was so great, that [one man] gathered up, among the filth of my house, all the fish-bones that he could find, which he dried and beat into a powder, to make bread thereof."

René Laudonnière, leader of the Huguenots at Fort Caroline,
writing about starvation in the settlement in 1565

15

The Spanish Arrive

Meanwhile, near the beginning of July 1565, Menéndez set sail from Spain. His **fleet** consisted of nineteen ships, leaving from various Spanish ports. Two-thirds of the ships met storms while crossing the Atlantic Ocean and only five ships eventually made their way to Florida. They carried about 500 soldiers, 200 sailors, and around 100 of what Menéndez called "useless people . . . married men, women, children, and **artisans**."

Lookouts sighted the Florida coastline on August 28, the day Catholics honor one of their most important saints, Saint Augustine. Menéndez sailed north along the coast for a few more days looking for a good harbor. He found one near the site of the Timucuan village of Seloy and named the place St. Augustine.

A huge steel cross, 208 feet (63 m) high, towers over St. Augustine Bay. It commemorates the first mass given by Father Francisco Lopez de Mendoza Grajales when the Spanish landed.

The Defeat of Fort Caroline

Angered and frightened by the arrival of the Spanish, the French colonists at Fort Caroline decided to attack. Leaving only a small **garrison** and a few ships behind, the French set sail for St. Augustine, where they arrived on September 11. They were just in time to see some of the Spanish ships departing, and the French ships chased after them. Observing this chase from St. Augustine, Menéndez thought that maybe he could turn the situation to his advantage. A storm was approaching, and it would be days, maybe even weeks, before the French could sail north back to Fort Caroline.

It was about 45 miles (72 kilometers) from St. Augustine to Fort Caroline across land. On September 18, 1565, Menéndez led his 500 soldiers north, guided by local Timucuans. When the Spanish reached Fort Caroline at dawn on September 20, they stormed the gate, catching the French unprepared. The fort was quickly captured.

Spanish soldiers attack Fort Caroline on September 20, 1565, killing about 130 of the French settlers. Another 45 escaped and about 50 women and children were taken prisoner.

The End of the French

Menéndez renamed Fort Caroline as San Mateo. He left some of his men there to guard the settlement and returned to St. Augustine. On September 28, Menéndez learned that the French ships that had chased his ships had been wrecked during the storm. Menéndez found and executed all the survivors except a handful who claimed to be Catholics. The French were no longer a threat in Florida.

Pedro Menéndez de Avilés (1519—1574)

Pedro Menéndez was born in Avilés on the northern coast of Spain. As a young man, he became an officer in the Spanish navy. Menéndez rose to the rank of admiral and gained fame fighting pirates. Appointed as governor of Florida, Menéndez set up his capital in St. Augustine. During the succeeding years, he continued to explore, found new cities, and fight on Spain's behalf. In 1574, Menéndez was in Spain assembling a fleet of ships when he developed a fever and died.

A Colony on Timucuan Land

While Menéndez and his soldiers fought the French, other colonists worked to convert Seloy's council house into a Spanish fort. It is not certain whether Seloy's residents stayed in St. Augustine or moved away, but at first the relationship between the Spanish and the Timucuans was friendly. The locals traded food and furs for metal tools and other European goods. In an effort to convert the Native people to Catholicism, the Spanish built a **mission** about half a mile (0.8 km) north of the fort. It was named *Nombre de Dios*, which means "name of God," and a Timucuan village grew up there.

The good relations didn't last, however. The Spanish soldiers showed little respect and simply took by force whatever it was they wanted, including Timucuan women. Some Timucuans remained cautiously friendly, but others began attacking any Spaniard who left the fort.

The first of many building projects begins at St. Augustine as men are shown laying out the town. In the background, a group clusters around the priest for religious services.

Quick Arrows

"The natives conducted their warfare in this wise: small groups lay in ambush to shower arrows on any stray Spaniard. . . . They are so sure of not being caught that they venture very close to the Christians before discharging their arrows. These arrows are loosed with such force that they pierce any clothing as well as coats of mail. So quick are the Indians in releasing the arrows that they can wait for a [gun] to be discharged at them, and then release four or five arrows in the interval during which the soldier reloads his piece."

Bartolomé Barrientos, Pedro Menéndez de Avilés, *1567*

Starvation

When food grew scarce, Menéndez took some of his soldiers and sailed to Havana, Cuba, the center of Caribbean trade. Menéndez sent supplies to St. Augustine, but did not return himself. As governor of Florida, he decided he needed to explore the coastline and establish other Spanish bases.

As supplies dwindled during the winter of 1565–66, people in St. Augustine began to starve. Several hundred soldiers simply deserted the town. They either joined the Timucuans or tried to find passage to Spanish cities in the Caribbean. Disease struck down many of the new colonists, although those that followed Timucuan advice to drink boiled **sassafras** tea instead of the local water seemed to stay well. St. Augustine lost almost half its original settlers to death or desertion that first winter.

Rebuilding

In May 1566, the Timucuan chiefdoms united to declare war on the Spanish and burned down the fort in St. Augustine. Menéndez returned to restore order and rebuild the fort and town, this time across the bay on Anastasia Island. He arranged for regular supplies to come from Havana. In early summer of 1566, a fleet of ships from Spain arrived, bringing more than a thousand new soldiers. With new supplies and the addition of more men, St. Augustine became more secure, and construction of the town continued.

Over the years, as one disaster after another struck St. Augustine, its houses were built and rebuilt. None of the houses built in the 1500s still exists. These dwellings in the town are typical of the houses built by the Spanish in the 1600s.

20

A Spanish Outpost

St. Augustine was more of an **outpost** than a settled community. It was laid out like a traditional Spanish town, however, with a central plaza surrounded by small houses. Narrow streets crisscrossed the area. Usually, the houses contained two rooms and sat on plots of land 44 feet by 88 feet (13.4 m by 26.8 m). Every house had its own well to supply water. The houses were half-timbered, meaning they were built using wooden frames covered with mud or clay. Their roofs were thatched.

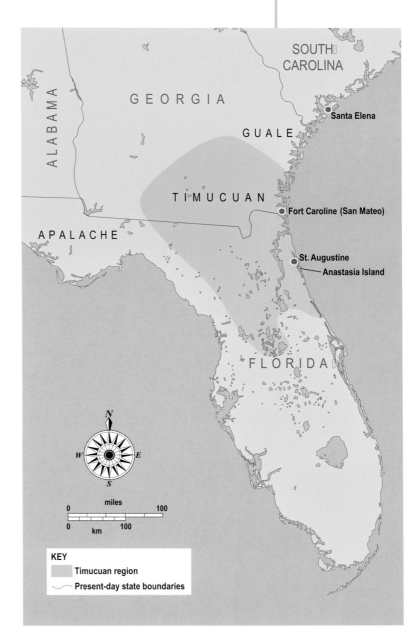

New Settlements

As soon as the town was secure, Menéndez left to continue his explorations. He mapped about 300 miles (480 km) of the North American coastline and started five more settlements, leaving about 150 of his soldiers in each place. He signed peace treaties with several Indian groups in southern Florida, but not with the Timucuans of northern Florida. They continued their attacks on St. Augustine and other Spanish settlements.

This map shows the land inhabited by the Timucuan people and their Guale and Apalache neighbors before the Spanish came. It also shows the early Spanish settlements of San Mateo (previously Fort Caroline), Santa Elena, and St. Augustine. Only St. Augustine survived into the 1600s.

New Colonists

By summer of 1568, San Mateo (previously Fort Caroline) was destroyed and the colonists at St. Augustine were in bad shape. Menéndez began recruiting colonists with skills for settling the land. In the spring of 1569, eighty new colonists settled in St. Augustine. They quickly built houses, planted crops, tended livestock, and engaged in trade; but disease, pirate attacks, and conflict with Indians soon claimed the lives of many new colonists.

Menéndez was convinced that Florida could generate great wealth by producing food and other goods to be sold in Europe. He sent for equipment to begin whaling expeditions and ordered the planting of wheat fields and vineyards. He also started cattle, pig, and sheep farming.

Survival

In 1572, the town was moved back across the bay and rebuilt on the mainland in its present location. By the early 1570s, pig farms and cornfields had been established. St. Augustine began to export natural resources in the form of lumber and sassafras root. The colony was developing a limited system of commerce.

A cornfield under a stormy sky in Florida. Corn was the staple food of the Native Florida people, and after a few years the Spanish settlers established their own fields for corn and other crops.

A group of Timucuans mount an attack on an early colony in Florida. The Native men were very skilled with the bow and arrow and had tactics suited to the environment. Their attacks were often successful in spite of the fact that the soldiers had guns.

Somehow, St. Augustine and one other settlement, Santa Elena, survived until Menéndez died in 1574. After his death, Hernando de Miranda, husband of Menéndez's daughter Catalina, became governor and settled in Santa Elena. He showed no interest in building up the colony and allowed Spanish officials to treat the Native people cruelly.

Peace Treaty

In 1576, Native Americans attacked the Spanish settlement at Santa Elena. The survivors, including Governor Miranda, fled to St. Augustine. The Native people then attacked there, too, destroying all the houses. Eighty men and one hundred women and children survived the attack and took refuge in the fort.

The Spanish **Council of the Indies** removed Miranda and appointed Menéndez's nephew, Pedro Menéndez Marquez, as Florida's new governor. Menéndez Marquez began rebuilding St. Augustine and finally arranged a peace treaty with the Timucuans. For the first time in a decade, there were friendly relations between St. Augustine and its nearest neighbors.

Poor Government

"I have suffered hunger, nudity and much misery, not because the land is so bad as they hold it to be, but due to the poor government it has had, and because their resources were too little to conquer so many people and such a great land. . . . What I say to Your Majesty about this land of which all the world says ill, is that it is a marvel of good, because there are most rich lands for tillage and stock-farms, powerful rivers of sweet water, great fertile plains and mountains."

Colonist Bartolomé Martínez, in a letter to King Philip II, February 17, 1577

Chapter 4

Life in St. Augustine

King Philip II ruled Spain from 1556 until his death in 1598. He also had ultimate authority over the vast areas of North and South America conquered and settled by his soldiers and priests. King Philip sent money and supplies to keep St. Augustine going.

Under the strong leadership of Pedro Menéndez Marquez, St. Augustine began to develop into a genuine community. By 1580, it was clear that St. Augustine not only would survive as a colony, but might even grow.

Government

The colony was ruled by the King of Spain and his Council of the Indies. They appointed the governor, who was in charge of both the townspeople and the military forces. The king also appointed three treasury officials to safeguard colony money and royal property.

The People of St. Augustine

In 1580, St. Augustine had a population of 275 colonists. Of these, 110 were soldiers, 20 were seamen, and 100 were women and children. The remaining 45 were priests, town officials, and craftspeople, such as carpenters and smiths.

Single men rarely owned their own houses. Most boarded with a family. Often they bartered their skills rather than paying in cash for food and lodging.

Because there were so few Spanish women, many men took Timucuan

The Plan

"He shall build and populate [within] three years two or three towns in the places and ports which seem to him the best. . . . He will place . . . at least ten or twelve [priests] of the order which seems best to him . . . that the Indians might be converted to our Holy Catholic faith and to the obedience of His Majesty. . . . He shall attempt to place, within the said three years, five hundred slaves for his service and for that of the people, in order that the towns might be built with more facility and the land might be cultivated. . . ."

Agreement between Spanish Council and Pedro Menéndez de Avilés,
signed by King Philip II, March 20, 1565

Men dressed as seventeenth-century Spanish soldiers interpret Spanish colonial history for visitors to St Augustine's ancient fort. Soldiers dominated St. Augustine in its early days as a military outpost.

women as their wives. In 1580, about one-fourth of the households included a Native American female. Within the next few decades, African slaves and convicts from Spain would also become a significant part of the population.

Laws in St. Augustine

Florida's "**Ordinances** of Government" established by Pedro Menéndez de Avilés in 1567 were North America's first European set of laws. They established a council for each Florida settlement and gave the council the power to collect taxes, try criminal cases, and assign plots of land. They also regulated the marketplace, establishing prices, weights, and measures.

The document gave directions for religious instruction and military discipline. The punishments it set out were harsh. Crimes such as failure to attend mass or follow military discipline could be punished by whippings or hard labor. Some crimes, such as **mutiny**, carried a death sentence.

The Town

In 1580, St. Augustine had a church and several shops. The fort was a two-story, rectangular wooden building. There were a number of **taverns**, and about a hundred houses had been built since the Indian attack in 1576. There was even a lighthouse on an island just off the coast, used to signal ships and watch for pirates.

How They Lived

St. Augustine's houses were built along narrow lanes. Most homes were half-timbered as before, but richer people added walls and floors made of pine boards. Kitchens were always separate to reduce smells, heat, and fire risk in the main house. Most houses looked out onto an open courtyard or garden in the back, and some had a stable in the courtyard for livestock. The stables may have doubled as outhouses.

The colonists dug wells, but they also collected water in large clay jars, called *tinajones*. These huge vessels could weigh as much as 800 pounds (360 kilograms). They were placed under the eaves of a house to catch the rainwater and buried partly underground to keep the water cool.

This room is in a reconstructed house in St. Augustine's Spanish Quarter. It shows visitors what living quarters were like in the colony in the early 1700s.

Food in St. Augustine

St. Augustine colonists traded with the Timucuans for food and raised some of their own. Families were assigned garden plots outside the town, where they grew vegetables. They planted fruit trees, usually oranges or figs, in their yards. The average diet included corn, beans, pumpkin, oranges, peaches, figs, and fish. The colonists also ate poultry, raccoons, opossums, and deer.

The rich could afford to import special treats such as chocolate or hazelnuts. They could also buy the meat of cattle and pigs raised in the colony. Poorer colonists could rarely afford to buy beef or pork. For most people, getting enough food to survive was a struggle.

Native people bring harvested food to a storehouse for winter supplies.

St. Augustine had the first public schools in North America north of Mexico. This schoolhouse in St. Augustine, built in 1763, is said to be the oldest in the United States.

Daily Life

The military presence in St. Augustine dominated the town. At the fort, soldiers on guard duty took six-hour watches, looking out for pirates, **privateers**, and any sign of attack from Native neighbors.

The Catholic religion was an important part of daily life in St. Augustine, and everyone attended church. Priests conducted daily masses and heard confession. They also established the first public schools in what would become the United States.

People in town could tell time by the changing of the guard or the ringing of the church bells. For most colonists, their day was devoted to chores. Crops were planted and tended, meals were cooked, and clothes were mended and washed. Storms might vary the routine as some colonists then searched the coast, looking for survivors and cargo from shipwrecks.

Ships made frequent trips to Cuba to trade lumber, food, and other goods for supplies. Although trade was established and life in St. Augustine became more settled, it was never very secure. Diseases still killed people, and sometimes there was not enough food.

Attacks on the Colony

During the time of Spain's colonization of the Americas, Spanish ships were constantly under attack by privateers. These were English, Dutch, or French adventurers encouraged by their governments to attack Spanish ships carrying goods from the colonies back to Europe.

Privateers also plundered Spanish settlements, and St. Augustine was attacked several times. The most devastating assault occurred in June of 1586. English adventurer Francis Drake had already plundered Cartagena in Colombia and the island of Santo Domingo when he decided to sail up the Florida coastline.

As soon as Drake's fleet of forty-two vessels was spotted, the women and children were sent to a nearby Timucuan village and the soldiers hid their cannons by burying them in sand. On June 7, Spanish soldiers forced the first English assault party to retreat, but Governor Menéndez Marquez realized that the large number of English invaders would eventually overwhelm them. He decided to abandon St. Augustine and ordered his men into the woods. Drake seized the town's money chest and allowed his men to loot the city. Spanish deserters showed the English where the cannons had been buried, and Drake took those, too. His men destroyed the gardens and orchards and burned all the houses.

This engraving of Francis Drake's assault on St. Augustine was made just after the attack. It was based on the drawings of an eyewitness, maybe even Drake himself. In the center, the English are firing at the fort from Anastasia Island. On the left, the English are entering the town.

These pieces of gold and other treasures come from a Spanish ship that sank off the coast of Cuba in 1590. The recovered items include gold nuggets and silver coins.

Natural Disasters

The Spanish refused to give up, and they rebuilt their town. It didn't last long. In 1599, fire swept through St. Augustine, burning down part of the town. Then a hurricane caused the sea to rise, and it flooded what was left. Undaunted, the Spanish rebuilt yet again.

Improving the City

"All I can say at present is that there are about 250 soldiers in this Garrison . . . they are good and well drilled and disciplined; that the Governor has planted and under cultivation many acres of land, which will be a great help in the sustenance of these people, who are mostly married, and whose small wages and rations given them does not suffice for their support. They certainly need this grain. Besides others, seeing the good results and what good land it is, are following the example and are clearing and planting fields. With the cutting down of the timber it has done away with the vast quantities of mosquitoes and has helped to improve the city, as one sees on all sides houses in course of construction."

St. Augustine colonist Redondo Villegas, letter to King Philip III of Spain, April 18, 1600

From 1576—when Santa Elena was abandoned—until 1698, St. Augustine was the only Spanish settlement in Florida apart from the missions. The town was still basically a military base, however. **Emigrants** from Spain to the colonies usually chose Mexico, the Caribbean, or South America. There they would find thriving economies and avoid hurricanes and attacks by pirates and Indians.

By 1700, therefore, the population of St. Augustine had grown to only about 1,400 or 1,500 people. Some had started ranches or farms outside the city limits, but most worked for the government, either as city officials or as soldiers.

This is a view of St. Augustine in 1673. It shows the growing town in the background on the left and the wooden fort on the right. Ships and boats of all kinds filled the port with activity.

The Missions

In the 1600s, priests were founding missions throughout northern Florida, but St. Augustine was their base. Missionaries were a common sight in the streets of the town.

A Duty to Convert

During the 1600s, St. Augustine continued to protect Spain's claim on Florida, and the city served as a supply base and guard for Spanish ships. The settlement's most lasting impact, however, was on the Native population. The Spanish believed it was their duty to convert the Native people to Catholicism. It was also an effective way of gaining control over them and acquiring a cheap source of labor for farming, mining, building, and domestic work.

Early attempts at conversion had been mostly unsuccessful. After Pedro Menéndez Marquez became governor, conversion became a priority. In the late 1500s, as missionaries began succeeding with the Timucuans, Spanish leaders decided to try to extend Spanish influence to the Guale and Apalache peoples. By 1655, there were seventy **friars** in Florida and many thousands of converted Indians. The friars had founded a string of ten missions along the east Florida coastline and more than thirty others inland.

Pledging Obedience

The friars' efforts focused on converting the chiefs. They knew if a chief converted, he would order his people to do so. The chiefs, required to pledge obedience to the Spanish king, thought that by converting they had acquired powerful allies. They did not always realize that they were in fact sacrificing their independence.

Bribes and Ceremonies

When a friar made his first contact with a Florida village, he tried to impress the villagers as much as possible. He wore his most ornate clothes and displayed paintings and sacred statues. Ceremonies used music, incense, candles, and worship of the cross. Friars also tried to win the people over with gifts of glass beads, clothing, tools, and food. Once chiefs accepted gifts, they often felt obliged to the missionaries, who used that advantage to talk Native people into converting.

Even chiefs who had not been visited by missionaries would sometimes travel to St. Augustine and offer their allegiance voluntarily. If they didn't, other villages would refuse to trade with them. Some people would leave their own, unconverted village to join one that had the advantage of support from the Spanish.

Being a Convert

Some people were genuine in their conversion to Catholicism. They saw the Spanish as powerful and thought that their god must be powerful also. Others agreed to be baptized simply to please the Spanish. In either case, most Native converts simply added Christian practices to their existing religious beliefs.

The cathedral in St. Augustine is built in the Spanish mission style. High up under the church bells is a statue of the Catholic saint that gave his name to the city.

33

The Timucuan, Guale, and Apalache people labored for the Spanish at any number of activities. This engraving from 1591 shows Native people hunting for gold in the gravel of a Florida streambed.

"Civilized" Living

"[Converts should be taught] to live in a civilized manner, clothed and wearing shoes . . . given the use of bread and wine and oil and many other essentials of life . . . silk, linen, horses, cattle, tools, and weapons, and all the rest that Spain has had. [They are to be] instructed in the trades and skills with which they might live richly."

Spanish orders regarding converts, "Royal Orders for New Discoveries of 1573," July 13, 1573

When Native people were baptized, they were given Spanish names. Their villages were also renamed in Spanish. European dress was encouraged, and over time, all Indian ceremonies and traditions were eliminated.

Tribute and Slavery

One aim of converting the Native population was to acquire slaves or cheap laborers for the Spanish. When the chiefs pledged obedience to the Spanish king, part of their agreement was that they would supply workers for various projects in St. Augustine. This was a system familiar to Florida people because lesser chiefs and their subjects paid **tribute** to great chiefs in the form of food and services. Throughout the mission period, Native people worked as laborers for the Spanish, planting crops, hauling supplies, and performing other menial labors.

Decline of the Mission System

In 1635, there were about 30,000 converts living in various missions. This number had fallen to 6,550 by 1680. Most of the decline was due to European diseases, such as smallpox. Native people, converted or not, died by the thousands.

Friars also faced rebellion among their converts. Native people resented the slavery that came with conversion. In particular, they protested at being used as beasts of burden, forced to carry supplies from the missions to St. Augustine or other places because there were no pack animals available. When protest turned to violence, Spanish soldiers dealt with the rebels severely, and many people were killed. Others moved to lands not controlled by the Spanish. By 1700, the mission system was barely functioning.

Slave Labor

"For lack of pack animals, the said Indians bring on their back and transport the fruits and goods of the land which are bartered and traded, . . . [Many refuse to be Christians] in order not to experience similar labor, from which it has resulted in some dying on the roads in times of cold [weather], and there was a Christian Indian woman who, having had a male child, killed him without baptism in order not to see him made a slave."

Royal Treasurer Don Joseph de Prado, in a petition to the governor of Florida, December 23, 1654

There were several rebellions by Native people against missions and missionaries. Here, men are shown gathering for a battle against European colonists. As their numbers dwindled due to disease and slavery, many groups in Florida united to strengthen their resistance.

35

Chapter 6

Florida Under Many Flags

Conflict with the British

By the early 1700s, the British had a number of colonies in North America along the Atlantic coast. As these colonies grew in strength, there was increasing tension between Britain and Spain. In the early 1700s, the British launched several attacks against St. Augustine and its fort, the Castillo San Marcos.

The British Take Over

From 1754 to 1763, the British and the French fought for control of North America in the French and Indian War. In 1762, Spain entered the war, siding with the French, but France surrendered soon after. During the war, Britain had captured the island of Cuba. To get it back, Spain agreed to give Florida to the British. As a result, nearly all of the Spanish colonists chose to move to Cuba.

This map shows how North America was divided between Spain and Britain in 1763 after France surrendered. British territory expanded greatly and now included Florida.

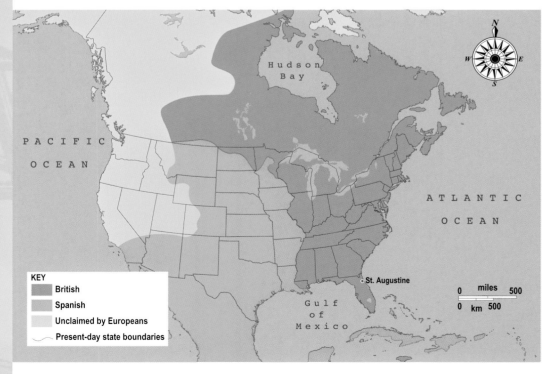

KEY
- British
- Spanish
- Unclaimed by Europeans
- Present-day state boundaries

The Castillo de San Marcos

Beginning in 1671, the construction of a new fort, the Castillo de San Marcos, was St. Augustine's most ambitious project. The fort's designer was Ignacio Daza, an engineer from Havana. The skilled craftsmen were mostly Spanish, and the unskilled workers were Timucuan, Guale, and Apalache laborers.

An aerial view of the Castillo de San Marcos.

The Castillo was built of *coquina*, a yellow stone formed from layers of seashells. The stone was taken from Anastasia Island, just off the shore of St. Augustine, and cut into building blocks. These were held together with a paste made from crushed oyster shells that hardened like cement.

The Castillo de San Marcos is square with **bastions** protruding from each corner. The walls are about 20 feet (6 m) high, and a deep moat surrounds the whole building. Cannons and **mortars** are perched around the fort. The only entrance is a narrow drawbridge over the moat on the side of the fort facing the town. Originally, it was thought it would take four years to complete the Castillo. In the end, it took twenty-three years, and the fort was not completed until 1695.

A bronze mortar that was added to the fort in 1724.

The British and Americans brought African slaves in large numbers to St. Augustine. This is the old slave market in St. Augustine, photographed in 1896 after slavery had been abolished by the United States.

The British governors hoped to create a **plantation** system in Florida, just as they had done in their colonies of Virginia, the Carolinas, and Georgia. To work on the plantations, the British brought in hundreds of African slaves. Few of the early plantations succeeded, but plantations and slavery eventually became part of life in Florida, as they were in the southern British colonies.

Fort Mose

During the early 1700s, African slaves from British colonies sometimes managed to escape to Florida. If they were willing to convert to the Catholic faith and join the military, the Spanish government declared them free. In 1738, a community for the former slaves, Gracia Real de Santa Teresa de Mose, was built about 2 miles (3 km) north of St. Augustine. Fort Mose, as it was usually known, was the first free black community in North America. About one hundred men, women, and children lived there. During a British attack in 1740, the fort was burned and its inhabitants moved to St. Augustine. In 1752, a second Fort Mose was built. It had twenty-two homes, a church, a house for the priests, and a lookout tower. The people prospered there until 1763, when they fled to Havana at the time of the British occupation.

An International City

The town struggled on. Britain could not recruit enough British colonists, so it encouraged people from other countries to come. As time passed, St. Augustine became a truly international city. In addition to the British, Africans, and Spanish, there were settlers from Greece, Italy, Germany, France, and the island of Minorca in the Mediterranean Sea.

After the Timucuan, Guale, and Apalache populations had been destroyed, the Spanish encouraged other Native peoples, including Creeks (from Alabama and Georgia) and Cherokees (from the southern Appalachians) to come to Florida to provide cheap labor. With so many cultures represented, the people of St. Augustine had to learn how to get along with those who were different from themselves.

The American Revolution

When the British colonies declared their independence and became the United States of America in 1776, Florida stayed loyal to Britain. St. Augustine became an important base for the British during the American Revolution. People from the United States who wanted to stay loyal to Britain flooded into the town. In addition, the British forces sent prisoners of war to be held in St. Augustine. In 1776, the population was about 6,000. By 1781, it had grown to about 17,000 people, more than half of whom were African slaves. Suddenly, the town was alive and prospering.

It was a shock when Britain surrendered to the United States in 1781. The citizens worried about what would happen next, and with good reason. Spain had helped the United States during the war and had gained control of western Florida. When the peace treaty ending the Revolutionary War was signed on September 3, 1783, the United States gave all of Florida back to Spain.

The flags along Charlotte Street reflect St. Augustine's international history. In the foreground is the British flag and behind it the flag of the United States. Just visible is the Cross of Burgundy, used by Spain from the early 1500s until 1785.

Spain made a treaty with the United States that handed over the territory of Florida to the Americans. This is the first page of the original document signed in 1819.

A Land of Frogs and Alligators

"Florida, sir, is not worth buying. It is a land of swamps, of quagmires, of frogs and alligators and mosquitoes! A man, sir, would not immigrate into Florida. No, sir! No man would immigrate into Florida—no, not from hell itself!"

Virginia Congressman John Randolph, during a debate over the acquisition of Florida in the House of Representatives, c. 1805

The Spanish Return

About three hundred British colonists stayed when the Spanish returned in 1783. Spain tried to persuade some of the Spanish who had lived there before to return, but few did. Once American settlers began moving south, ignoring the Florida border, there were soon more English-speaking settlers in St. Augustine than Spanish-speaking ones. It wasn't long before U.S. leaders began debating whether the United States should try to purchase the land of Florida from Spain.

St. Augustine, still raided by pirates and Indians, was a drain on Spanish resources. Spain decided to concentrate on wealthier regions and, in 1819, gave Florida to the United States. In return, the United States took care of $5 million in claims against Spain by paying off Americans whose ships had been attacked by Spanish privateers. On July 10, 1821, the U.S. flag flew over the Castillo de San Marcos, which was renamed as Fort Marion in 1825.

The Civil War

Florida became a state in 1845. When the Civil War began in 1861, Florida joined the Confederate States of America, and a Confederate flag flew over Fort Marion. In 1862, the Union captured a city just north of St. Augustine and then sailed south. When the Confederate soldiers saw them approaching, they abandoned the city. Union forces occupied Fort Marion, and the U.S. flag flew there once again.

The Seminole Wars

The Seminoles of Florida were **descendants** mostly of Creek Indians but also of African people who had run away from slavery in the British colonies. The Spanish gave them the name Seminole, which means "wild one" or "runaway." In 1817, about five thousand Seminole people were living in northern Florida.

White Americans had attacked Seminole towns, taking the people as slaves, even when Florida was still Spanish. After Florida became U.S. territory, Americans tried to take Seminole land by force. The Seminoles fiercely resisted being enslaved and forced off their land. As a result, there were several periods of war between 1817 and 1858.

A group of Seminole people in the Florida Everglades in the 1930s.

The Seminoles first surrendered in 1842, and most of them were forced to move to Oklahoma. A few hundred managed to escape into the Everglades of southern Florida. In a conflict lasting from 1855 to 1858, about 250 of these fugitives were captured and forced to leave. Those who remained did not sign a peace treaty with the United States until 1935.

Conclusion

The Ponce de León Hotel was built by Henry Flagler and is typical of the extravagant architecture of the 1880s. The building is now the home of Flagler College.

American Identity

"We Americans have yet to really learn our own antecedents, and sort them, to unify them. . . . To that composite American identity of the future, Spanish character will supply some of the most needed parts. No stock shows a grander historic retrospect—grander in religiousness and loyalty, or for patriotism, courage, decorum, gravity and honor."

American poet Walt Whitman,
writing about Spanish settlement in
North America, July 20, 1883

The Flagler Era

In 1884, a millionaire named Henry Morrison Flagler decided to turn St. Augustine into a resort for rich tourists. Huge hotels and churches were built, and the town was promoted as a desirable place. People flocked there, attracted by the warm weather, the beaches, and the historic sites. People suffering from illnesses, especially tuberculosis, came to improve their health. Toward the end of the nineteenth century, the town was busy with plays, concerts, dances, golf, tennis, and water sports.

St. Augustine Today

Beginning in the 1930s, the city government turned its attention to restoring and preserving the historic sites. St. Augustine is now a thriving city. Thousands of tourists visit its historic sites every year. The restored Spanish Quarter is a living museum with eight houses shown as they were in the 1740s. Visitors can see how the Spanish colonists lived during that time. Town guides, dressed in colonial costumes, demonstrate how tasks such as candle-making, blacksmithing, and gardening were done.

In St. Augustine, visitors can view everything from humble cottages to Spanish Renaissance mansions with their colorful red-tile roofs to the massive Castillo de San Marcos. Several festivals, such as Blessing of the Fleet on Easter Sunday, recall the history of the city.

The Legacy of St. Augustine

St. Augustine is of historic significance as the oldest existing European settlement in North America. The city's architecture, museums, and many festivals help preserve Spanish heritage and custom. Its later, more international culture is a model for American society.

The Spanish colonists and soldiers who founded the city demonstrated courage and determination, but they also showed great **arrogance** and greed. Like other European colonists, they took the land by force and compelled the Native people living there to adopt a foreign lifestyle and customs. Although they brought new traditions with them, they destroyed the Timucuan people and the original Native culture of Florida.

A coat of arms bearing the Spanish emblem is carved in stone and mounted on the walls of the Castillo de San Marcos.

Time Line

1513	April 2: Juan Ponce de León lands in Florida.
1564	French Huguenots settle in northern Florida and build Fort Caroline.
1565	March 20: King Philip II of Spain authorizes Pedro Menéndez de Avilés to colonize Florida.
	September 8: Spanish colonists land in Florida and occupy Timucuan village of Seloy.
	September 20: Menéndez and his soldiers defeat French at Fort Caroline and capture fort.
1566	St. Augustine is moved across St. Augustine Bay and rebuilt on Anastasia Island.
1567	Menéndez issues Ordinances of Government.
1572	St. Augustine is moved back to mainland and rebuilt.
1574	Pedro Menéndez dies and Hernando de Miranda is appointed governor of Florida.
1576	Native Americans attack and destroy Santa Elena and St. Augustine. Pedro Menéndez Marquez is appointed governor of Florida.
1586	June 7–8: English fleet under Francis Drake attacks and burns St. Augustine.
1587	Growth of Florida mission movement begins.
1599	Fire and flooding destroy most of St. Augustine.
1671	Work begins on Castillo de San Marcos.
1738	Fort Mose is established.
1763	Britain takes over Florida from Spain.
1781	British surrender to United States in Revolutionary War.
1783	Florida returns to Spanish rule.
1817	First Seminole War begins.
1819	Spain gives Florida to the United States.
1825	Castillo de San Marcos is renamed Fort Marion.
1835	Second Seminole War begins.
1845	Florida becomes a state.
1855	Third Seminole War begins.
1861	Florida joins the Confederate States of America.
1862	March 11: United States retakes St. Augustine.
1942	Fort Marion's name is restored to Castillo de San Marcos.

Glossary

arrogance: behavior demonstrating a belief in one's own superiority.

artisan: craftsperson.

bastion: stronghold or, in the case of the Castillo de San Marcos, part that sticks out of a fort or other stronghold.

census: official population count.

colony: settlement, area, or country owned or controlled by another nation.

Council of the Indies: governing body of Spanish colonies in the Americas.

descendant: person who comes in a later generation in a family. This could be a grandchild or someone many generations and hundreds of years later.

economy: system of producing and distributing goods and services.

emigrant: person who leaves his or her place of residence to go and live somewhere else.

empire: political power that controls large territory, usually consisting of colonies or other nations.

farrier: person who shoes horses.

fleet: group of ships under a single command.

friar: member of a Catholic religious order who takes vows of poverty, chastity and devotion to God's work.

garrison: military post; also the troops stationed at a military post.

mission: complex built to establish Spanish settlement and for converting and exploiting the labor of Native Americans.

mortar: type of cannon with a short barrel, used for firing shells at an enemy.

mutiny: rebellion against a superior officer by soldiers or sailors.

natural resources: naturally occurring materials, such as wood, oil, and gold, that can be used or sold.

ordinance: local rule or law.

outpost: outlying settlement. It could be a smaller, distant part of a main settlement or a military or trading post.

panhandle: narrow strip of land sticking out of a larger area, like a handle sticks out of a pan. Florida, Texas, and Oklahoma are all states with panhandles.

plantation: large farm growing cash crops and employing a large number of slaves or laborers.

privateer: privately owned ship that attacks enemy ships; also a sailor who serves on such a ship.

sapling: young tree small enough to have a thin, bendable trunk.

sassafras: type of tree, the root and bark of which are used to flavor drinks.

tavern: place where people went to drink alcohol, like a bar today.

thatch: dried grasses or leaves woven tightly together to make roofing material.

tribute: payment by group or nation to a ruling nation, person, or protector.

Further Information

Books

Binns, Tristan Boyer. *St. Augustine* (Visiting the Past). Heinemann Library, 2001.

Chui, Patricia and Jean Craven. *Florida: the Sunshine State* (World Almanac Library of the States). World Almanac Library, 2002.

Manning, Ruth. *Juan Ponce de León* (Groundbreakers). Heinemann Library, 2000.

Manucy, Albert C. *Menéndez : Pedro Menéndez de Avilés, Captain General of the Ocean Sea*. Pineapple Press, 1992.

McCarthy, Kevin M. *Native Americans in Florida*. Pineapple Press, 1999.

Sita, Lisa. *Indians of the Northeast: Traditions, History, Legends, and Life* (Native Americans). Gareth Stevens, 2000.

Web Sites

www.ancientnative.org Heritage of the Ancient Ones, an organization devoted to preserving the history of Florida's Native people, offers lots of information about the Timucuan and other groups.

www.flmnh.ufl.edu Florida Museum of Natural History has an online exhibition that traces St. Augustine's history through archaeological finds.

www.nps/gov/casa Information about and pictures of the Castillo de San Marcos from the National Park Service, with good links to web sites of other historical sites in Florida.

Useful Addresses

Castillo de San Marcos National Monument
National Park Service
1 Castillo Drive East
St. Augustine, FL 32084
Telephone: (904) 829-6506

St. Augustine Historical Society
271 Charlotte Street
St. Augustine, FL 32084
Telephone: (904) 824-2872

Index

Page numbers in *italics* indicate maps and diagrams. Page numbers in **bold** indicate other illustrations.